THE
MURDERED
WOMAN:
A DOUBLE
FEATURE

ESSENTIAL TRANSLATIONS SERIES 58

ONTARIO ARTS COUNCIL
CONSEIL DES ARTS DE L'ONTARIO
an Ontario government agency
un organisme du gouvernement de l'Ontario

Ontario 🏵

Canada Council   Conseil des arts
for the Arts   du Canada

Guernica Editions Inc. acknowledges the support of
the Canada Council for the Arts and the Ontario Arts Council.
The Ontario Arts Council is an agency of the Government of Ontario.
We acknowledge the financial support of the Government of Canada through
the National Translation Program for Book Publishing, an initiative
of the *Roadmap for Canada's Official Languages 2013-2018:
Education, Immigration, Communities*, for our translation activities.
We acknowledge the financial support of the Government of Canada.
Nous reconnaissons l'appui financier du gouvernement du Canada.

CAROLE DAVID

THE MURDERED WOMAN:
A DOUBLE FEATURE

Translated by
Donald Winkler

GUERNICA
EDITIONS

TORONTO • CHICAGO
BUFFALO • LANCASTER (U.K.)
2024

Guernica Founder: Antonio D'Alfonso

Michael Mirolla, editor
Cover and interior design: Rafael Chimicatti
Guernica Editions Inc.
1241 Marble Rock Rd., Gananoque (ON), Canada K7G 2V4
2250 Military Road, Tonawanda, N.Y. 14150-6000 U.S.A.
www.guernicaeditions.com

Distributors:
Independent Publishers Group (IPG)
600 North Pulaski Road, Chicago IL 60624
University of Toronto Press Distribution (UTP)
5201 Dufferin Street, Toronto (ON), Canada M3H 5T8

First edition.
Printed in Canada.

Legal Deposit—Third Quarter
Library of Congress Catalog Card Number: 2024930319
Library and Archives Canada Cataloguing in Publication
Title: The murdered woman : a double feature / Carole David ;
translated by Donald Winkler.
Other titles: Programme double de la femme tué. English .
Names: David, Carole, author. | Winkler, Donald, translator.
Series: Essential translations series ; 58.
Description: First edition. | Series statement: Essential translations series ; 58
Translation of: Le Programme double de la femme tué.
Identifiers: Canadiana 20240287193 | ISBN 9781771838955 (softcover)
Subjects: LCGFT: Poetry.
Classification: LCC PS8557.A77 P7613 2024 | DDC C841/.54—dc23

In memory of François Hébert

*If this were enough: to arrive somewhere
while uttering flawlessly its name, to be at home.*
—Antonella Anedda, *For a New Winter*

CONTENTS

VIRTUE

I wander the streets of Rome with as my sole guide my telephone's raw light. Beatrice, the beautiful parricide, condemned by the popes' courts, holds her decapitated head in her hands on the Ponte Sant'Angelo. She is seeking her mother-in-law and her brothers. Archangel Michael has spurned her, turned aside as she passed. The following day I meet her at the Palazzo Barberini. From within a fabled canvas, she smiles out at me on the eve of her augured death. Then I roam the hallways of her father's castle.

The night of September 11 to 12, 2019

The rodents have overrun
the prideful capital
have joined forces with the irises
for a new life
my daily task
is to lose sight of them
I was this pillaged house
that is no longer my own
no one awaits me
my affliction takes pride of place
pending widowhood
I erect a mortuary cloister

In the mouth three diamonds
buried burned
I caught up with you
at the body farm
you remind me of my pledge
once freed from hell
I hear the she-wolf
croon her gilded songs
I am not her offspring
I dwell in a princely fable
there where the wave breathes me in

The nearness of the desert
wraps us round
lets the garlands of gaudy bulbs
pilot us towards the sky
an inward Italy is pure invention
its fabled creatures encage us
bequeathing no poem
no bequest

As lofty as the obelisks
the barbarous she-pope shows herself
haloed by a cloud of insects
this will be the triumphal entry
between Cestius' pyramid
and the ancient abattoir
an unsought sorrow
ossifies
despite the lush abundance

I chose
a tomb at random
bereft of ornament
I made it mine
marble excesses
hosted the cypresses
whose roots had rejoined the skies
as for the amphoras, they gave shelter
to the remnants of corals and slaves

The first hour through the maze
I am propelled far from the forest
flowered cassocks in the second person
counselling tragedy
I strip myself down
my weary castle takes form
amid a fauvist colony
caryatids summoned
back to life
are not palm trees
limbs of the Lord?

At the height of day
refolding the same décor
I eye you
colonized derelicts
somnolent wraiths
we steer our way
Caesar hands me back his bastards
his scaly women
those who act badly
who dance on the bridge
arms flung out
fetid flesh suits me

In the myth's depths
the courtesans leave their masks behind
on the consoles
head down alabaster corridors
waltz at the windows by night
weigh on my mind
the villa admits to its crimes

ANATOMY

After the rape she nurtures a project, that of a Madonna who would carry another's child. She refused a nun's garb, fled her chaperone, her brothers and her sisters. The knife and the paintbrush, emblems for the future. "The world is not a hued palette," she murmurs. All at once, I saw the blood spurt.

Galleria Spada with the painter
Artemisia Gentileschi, October 2019

It may be that *the spiritual application of black*[1]
has silenced this scene
the sentence pronounced with theatrical flare
believe me, I free figures from their mold
my instruments intone
an abstract of the carrion to come
the embrace, a tardy conversion

---

1 Yannick Haenel,
The Caravaggio Solitude

Among the shades
I am pledged
to metallic ruins
those modern volcanos
sulfurous but infused
with what will ease the ire of emperors
my noxious vocation
has its beginnings in the early morning
I assemble the fires
my speckled hands are vines
I come forth from the fresco
to which I've been assigned

Indolent, Caravaggio's sons
serve liquid prey
at table
princes back to front undone
honoured and nonchalant
I thank them by name
when night comes
I am chaos still
my meanness makes no sound

The ocean pounds the cliff
they tumble one by one
sated cherubs
slumped on the ground in the four winds
let them impel themselves
bereft of rest
I will bear their relics
like a radiance

My sister at this elevation
back bared, improbable hairdo
a motif shifting with the light
obsessed, I move room to room
throw myself at criss-crossed poles
this painting, I make of it a dwelling
the expert, she has dissected royal corpses
has opened their organs
to paradise

A figure painted in the act of death
with her, I flee
inns
derelict *insulae*
the once sequestered nuns
join our pack
so many bones broken
by the master of perspective
because faith is an aching question

TORMENT

What I know of her, a murdered countess, aunt of Giuseppe Tomasa di Lampedusa, author of *The Leopard*, found in room number 8 of a disreputable hotel, now vanished. The first documented Italian femicide. I turn in circles, go up and down from level to level in the railroad station. I lose my way. "In the past, gypsies camped out on the square," my friend tells me. I waited for her in front of Rome's McDonald's. A coffee and a *cornetto*, one euro.

> *Giulia Trigona went to her death*
> *near the Termini station in March, 1911*

If he had thought otherwise
the assassin would have lured her elsewhere
perhaps to a transfigured headland
his bait, a crown deposited on the bed
a fleeting dream
the horror set in for a brief instant
before her corpse locked away the calamity

I take in the double feature
of the murdered woman
bearing in on her image
nameless she turns the weapon on herself
what was taken from her is there on the screen
crimson letters, sub-titles
the screen fissures
you are you even before you
grow into understanding you
are not anyone, worthless,
not worth you[2]
repeated, the streaming, the spartan lesson

2 Claudia Rankine
Citizen – An American Ballad

The last spark
that's what this mild winter wrests from me
I close the border
I hue to each line
eternity precedes
for some unknown reason
the tales of decapitation
those tumbledown skulls
fêted at cocktail hour
la donna non è gente[3]

---

3 Peasant proverb: "The lady is no one."

The following dawn
I will become
to judge by my age
a mosaic secretly pieced together
a scene prefaced by forgetfulness
a vegetal décor
someone dictates songs to me
my minor home overrun
by boars
here am I set down upon the water

They sport stale furs
warm themselves around an ersatz fire
their mouldering voices
tender fraudulent cigarettes
scents of doomed emanations
my own reflection benumbed
we eye each other before reaching port
the city stands tall like a stupor
I will return there

SHIPWRECK

A stranger approaches a young woman whose soul is seasick, as are the objects at hand. She stands before him, a likeness that has talked lengthily to the moon, her sole companion. "Memory is a war zone, a mine field," she says.

On a ferry somewhere between Genoa and Palermo during the years of lead.

Reconstituted from flecks of gold
the refractory faith sparks no memories
I could swear that the stones talk
and bear within them the hour of death
I chose to spurn
via Caetani[4]
long before returning
to tender it an allegory

---

4 The lifeless body of Aldo Moro, executed by the Red Brigades in 1978, was found in the trunk of a Renault parked on that street.

The captive women have fled their island
those toppled sites with their black façades
they want to die without any fuss
at dawn on the last day
imbued with gravitas
they hurdle obstacles
gain the suburban sprawl
leave me alone with the stars

You think I am dead, torn asunder
a vestal virgin become at carnival time
a sombre angular silhouette
I don't remember the person
in whose name I signed
the terrorist untimely born

The communist with the blissful face rang my bell
in his hands the building's lyrical archives
why did the woman next door tell the worker
no one was home where I lived?
why were the windows stacked up during my absence?
what man sowed elephants and bats?
he who will assume my father's shape

John and Paul, American fops,
sold off their hearts
in exchange for poisoned sugar
one of them returns the next day
to excise his enemy's thorax
high on the seventh hill
a field of honour
the vine radiant, blood spilled
the family mourns its gored boys

The site of my loss and consolation
an antique city
where only mazes remain
nothing precedes me
I am the heir of unanswered prayers
imbued with the breath of penitents
the man from the ferry returns
so I hold myself close

Monica Vitti advances
along with thin young girls in high heels
they march in procession brandishing their fists
a former warlord rises from the riverbanks
comes out of the swamps
passes out tracts, sharp-edged words
while I immured in the garden
conjure them

REQUIEM

The octopus course consumed, her husband eyes her. Between them there is the matter of Argentina, a forced exile. She approaches my table and bares her forearm, with its homicidal tattoo. The illicit word resurfaces. She is the barbed wire girl fleeing time, setting her baggage down at my feet.

Two o'clock, Ristorante Eden, Monteverde

It is a sign that God haunts this town
I no longer ask if he exists
I avoid revealing his nature
even if I've renounced him
his soldiers push me back
to where I shut myself off
in the sunless workshop with its cactuses
the snails stand guard
from church to church
I begin to infiltrate
the far corner

The Virgin of Parto throws open her closet to me
the childbirth gifts pile up
the offerings proliferate
how to resist
what garment to choose?
which would make me look nubile?
garbed in a shawl
I attend the service
once, I'd sacrificed myself
bearing children
whose mother I was not
the cunning fathers thanked me

A drama shows its face
the fortune tellers charm me
a lush world
I stalk the dice throwers
in the thick fog
the Door of Angels opens
the actresses' murmurings revive
my skin that after all
is consigned to a lineage of silence

My foundering was a dark river that every day
caught me in its spate's grip
I called for help, it did not come
somewhere in Buenos Aires
I am dead
how to know if I have returned
you will find in my language no fait accompli

Maria Stella bears down on the last details
gathering up past lives
laying down flowers on abandoned rafts
the result is conclusive
the plague-stricken craving affection
quit the pyramid
she leads them
through coastal swamps
to the outflow

Each nuance owns its sorrow
grey frightens me no more
the olive tree upon glass shards
asks me to dance
with a muddied trollop
what is violet eats away at my lungs
an ancestral talisman
whose exact replica I am

This morning, I wake
depleting the light
proof of my abjection
the courtyard path
leads to the building's door
a famous writer lived here
her wretched personae
are laid into the threshold
a gloomy spectacle

Her smile toothless
she comes near
what attends us
is the sound of soldiers' boots
she dwelt in a bookstore
as one sleeps at a friend's
who will rape you
when the lights go out
"I envy you," she tells me.

ALTARPIECE

This other murdered woman who sometimes wears my face paces the *piazza* and takes shelter in the cinema. On the screen, our tiniest parts are nearing death. When she returns, children are bursting through the emergency exits, grabbing all the seats. They view the world.

In memory of Santa Scorese, murdered
on March 16th, 1991, in Bari, Puglia.

No matter
if I come to a standstill
estranged from the exiled goddesses
nearing the age of twenty
I am unreconciled to my execution
throwing off my orange halo
the voice of the wolf, its pronoun
fleshing out before my eyes

Spurred towards purgatories
as chilling
as ourselves afoot
stripped of our rags
poised for the milk-white moon's return
the waves have reached us
rotting algae alight
on our mouths
we traverse the dusk

Before the death throes
will we be revived
ask the weak
in the On-High's name
I spit
I ask forgiveness
I return to the Field of Flowers
that you have forgotten, Amorremio
preferring our shipwreck
we do not say love, we take possession
santa subito[5], by way of her martyrdom, I rejoice

---

5 A Latin phrase, "Canonize her immediately," and a documen-
tary by Alessandro Piva on the femicide that took place in Puglia
in 1991.

The rain begins again to fall
on second thought, the spectacle of the dead
accords with that of the living
a few years hence, I will eat
at this familial restaurant table
a drowned girl will take the order
before Giordano Bruno's pyre
the fire has spared me

I return to the scenes
of another crime
let us close our eyes
await a new miracle
the sanctified one garbed in blue
her bottle of Vecchia Romagna slung over her shoulder
runs in front of the fountain
the carnivorous flowers invade her

The revolution has entered into her
its deadly manifestation consists
in drinking poisons brewed
north of the hills
so far from so near to
what was its dynasty
a murky tide bursts forth
as did the events
ending in massacre

MAGIC

Her having arrived on her bicycle, I will call her Ninetta. Fierce and rebellious, she defies me. Her face defines itself little by little. I am not at home, well yes, perhaps. A stone sky is clothed in emptiness. Someone sent the messenger onto the square. I am surrounded by a ring of fire.

Afternoon, August 12 2019, towards the South

An orphan at the term of a Christian journey
I've been abducted by two green parrots
they know nothing of my anatomy
in the sun's service they have traversed
arcades, their venous system
seeking sustenance
as for me, I have summoned
to the aviary another world
dogs, coyotes, and indifferent foxes

The potion once ingested
our descendance becomes
a thriving and vibrant tomb
eternities have been undone
so we may arrive just so at home
the swan floats over the ruptured portmanteau

The Virgin swabbed clean
her Rolexes hocked
at the pawn shop
asking the price
I probe
the *cafone's* history
animals slaughtered
at a holy ceremony
necklaces ripped away
guts hung high
that done, the men
huddle around the victims
their blindness gaining ground

A probe, a shadow
for the shattered moon
improbable alleyways
close me in
someone is whispering behind my back
his merciful knife betraying him
a deaf and dumb sweltering
my life preserved intact
it is written
a rose window speaking volumes

Our holy family fled the burial grounds
and the abstract concrete sculptures
it sits at terrace tables
recalls we're from deep in the South
where our insurrections were born
there's a trademark brightness I've come to love
on the archaeological worksite
while appearing from nowhere
a guard gathers up gold leaves

Her dress borrowed
from other squalls than her own
a declination of particles
at sunrise
she presents herself
a deposed empress
a captive
her dowry is our destitution

I've given up any thought of finding her
a broken and empty shell
at first she worked in the fields
got herself pregnant by the landowner
more recently turned herself into a milliner
I visited the store
the same models as sold at the hotel
I did not want to climb to the castle
for fear of encountering her

The men play at *scopa*
they talk loudly
we photograph them without their consent
the girl behind the counter resembles
lost cousins
his face buried in a notebook
a young man sketches
spared by the sun
we seek what we have been

RESURRECTION

On the shore of Lake Albano, fishers find the headless body of Antonietta Longo. She had left her Sicilian village and worked as a servant in Rome. We were born on the same date, thirty years apart. Her head has vanished. It may have served in a ceremony or been offered up on an altar.

Castel Gandolfo, July 10, 1955

Over the low hills
a sacrifice takes place
in the presence of a crucifix
snared, I went with her
into a space open to distances
the bronze saints avert their faces
our cries are ignored
a man approaches
holding an electric candle
proceeds to the ablation of ovaries

Stripped of her goods
a newspaper set down
upon her legs, her torso
she had been flesh entire
in the service of humanity
tripped up by a bottomless darkness
on waking
the nymphs hail her resurrection

I fell down dead
awash in the absence of kisses
volcanic waters live forever
a sacristan, a mechanic
will find me cradled
in a bed of rocks
they will say
I lost my head
for love

Rome, July 2019 – Montreal, April 2021

ABOUT THE AUTHOR

Born in the Montreal neighbourhood of Rose-mont, CAROLE DAVID holds a doctorate in French Studies. For many years she was a professor of literature at the college level and now devotes herself entirely to writing. Her work has been awarded a number of important prizes, including the Prix Athanase-David in 2020. Her books have been translated into English and Italian.

ABOUT THE TRANSLATOR

DONALD WINKLER was born in Winnipeg and moved to Montreal in the mid-sixties, where over the years he pursued parallel careers as a director of cultural documentaries and as a translator of Quebec fiction, non-fiction and poetry. He is a three-time winner of the Governor General's Award for French to English translation and has been a finalist for that prize on three other occasions.

Printed by Imprimerie Gauvin
Gatineau, Québec